A *Beautiful* ROOM WILL CHANGE YOUR LIFE:

YOUR PERSONAL GUIDE TO COLOR

sixth&spring books

233 Spring Street
New York, NY 10013

1 3 5 7 9 10 8 6 4 2

Library of Congress Control Number: 2004108045

ISBN 1-931543-74-7

All paint colors and furnishings are current at time of publication.

Manufactured in China

Photographs by
Alderman Studios

Cover by
Michael Church Photography

Text by
Kimberley Wray

A *Beautiful* ROOM WILL CHANGE YOUR LIFE:

YOUR PERSONAL GUIDE TO COLOR

by Connie Post

acknowledgements

Finger Furniture

Nebraska Furniture Mart

Roomful Express

The Sherwin-Williams Company

Alderman Studios

contents

PROLOGUE

prologue

Throughout my career as a designer, I've realized that we all have a natural relationship with color built right into who we are as people. It's a relationship that begins forming almost as soon as we begin to experience the world around us.

This natural relationship with color actually starts in the crib the first time our tiny fingers examine a small toy, often in a bright primary like red (believed to be the first color babies recognize) or yellow. Later, we may discover the cool freshness of green as we attempt to crawl across an inviting expanse of lawn, the unexpected, icy coolness of white with our first winter snow, or the wonder of blue as we stretch upward, dazzled by a summer sky.

Do you remember the sheer joy you felt as a child when someone handed you a brand new box of crayons? How you just had to try out every one? Well, I've noticed something throughout my career as a design professional: As we age, too many people lose the sense of pleasure that comes from personal expression and splashing the world around us with glorious swathes of color. Soon the child's joy is replaced by the adult's fear of making mistakes. We learn to play it safe (remember how somebody said not to color outside the lines?).

The result is that most homes in America today are awash in a sea of neutrals. White walls, beige carpets, vanilla every-thing. Now, don't get me wrong. Neutrals have their place, as you'll see as we move along our colorful journey. But the fact is that most people choose neutrals, not because they're in the mood for nude (see page 25), but because they fear making a costly decorating mistake.

That's sad. Because the truth is, we humans respond to color in the most positive sense. In the stressed-out world we inhabit as adults, color has the power to change our moods (ever felt blue, been green with envy, or seen red? You get the idea…), and even to make us happy. In fact, when we surround ourselves by the hues that make us happy, color can act as a restorative element in our lives—brightening our outlook and bringing out the natural beauty in both ourselves and in our environments.

This in mind, you might say that my goal in writing this book is to help people create beautiful and colorful spaces for themselves and their families. I truly believe that a beautiful home enhances how everyone inside it feels. It is the one, true, safe place to escape the world's pressures. I believe in my soul, that a beautiful room will change your life.

BEGINNINGS
BEGINNINGS
BEGINNINGS
BEGINNINGS
BEGINNINGS
BEGINNINGS
BEGINNINGS

beginnings

We all have a sense of creativity instilled within us. You may not believe it at this very moment, and you may not think your living space reflects it, but you're already a decorator. Think about it: You started with a bare environment…a room, maybe two, maybe a whole house, and you began to dress the nakedness. Maybe you started with an heirloom that had been passed down through your family that you could never imagine living without. Maybe you found a pretty area rug at the local discount store when money was tight. Whatever the case, and wherever you are in the process, please take heart in the fact that we all started somewhere, with something, and began to create what we hoped would be the perfect picture. And, if you are a college student reading this book sitting on a milk crate in an empty dorm room, or newly divorced or displaced by the circumstances of life for whatever reason, know that you are not the first to begin with nothing of any significance.

neutrals

Puffs of clouds, the wing of a dove, a mother's pearls and a father's starched shirt, frost in winter or a budding dogwood in spring, the gown of a virginal bride or a baby at christening. White in all its myriad variations is clean and immaculate, pure in heart and spirit. Like a porch light that welcomes us home in the darkness, or a cold glass of milk after a cookie, white comforts, calms, and refreshes. White inspires too, whether a sheet of paper awaiting the writer's ink or the artist's brush, or a block of marble from which a sculptor may set an angel free.

As wonderful as white can be, studies show we often choose it for the wrong reason. Fearing a costly decorating mistake, we surround ourselves with all manner of white walls, or beige, creating houses swathed in sand and fog.

Like white, the solution is simplicity itself. You can take a bleached out, neutral palette from bland to beautiful by warming it up with earthy tones like cream, bisque, straw, bread, butterscotch, caramel, coffee, and yes, chocolate. (Yum!)

Are you in the mood to go nude? Neutrals are classic colors with staying power, so they are a practical choice if you want a look that will last.

Did you know?

The very definition of neutral is that it matches well with most other colors or shades and the advantage of using a neutral as the main color of any room is simply flexibility. Neutral upholstered furniture affords you the opportunity to change the feeling of a room with colorful pillows and throws, along with the ability to add seasonal changes like prints in spring or autumn leaves in the fall. (Not to mention colorful holiday decorations!). Neutral walls allow for changes in drapery and window treatments too. A flash of color in artwork, and voila!, you've got an all-new room and a new attitude toward life. With neutrals, you can change on a whim.

Right: Simple, beige upholstery looks movie star glamorous against walls painted in Virtual Taupe. Accent colors Basket Beige and Rice Grain (above) work well too.

See Paint Index, page 133.

A lot of people just like white and can't deal with color on their walls. If you're one of them, remember that there are many different shades of white, and the coldness of a pure white can be difficult to live with for a long time. Scientifically speaking, a human's eye is actually programmed to seek out color. This means that if our surroundings are too neutral, we subconsciously begin to look for color. Warm up your white wall paint by adding a touch of green, blue, or yellow and save the stark white for trim. While there's nothing like living in neutral, a dash of color adds interest.

Debating what color to choose for the walls in your hallways or have a small space that needs brightening? The whiter shades of pale are an especially good choice for narrow areas without windows because they reflect available light. Shades in the cream, buff or buttermilk family will help keep your spirits sunny, as will eggshells and pearls, alabasters and ivories.

DESIGN TIP

No beautiful room is complete without framed art and where one piece looks great, two are often even better. When hanging a pair of companion prints (opposite page), never leave a space between the frames exceeding six inches, and hang your pictures no higher than twelve inches above the top of your sofa. If you have more wall décor to display on other walls in the room, make sure that the tops or bottoms of all your frames are aligned around the room to prevent visual chaos. Otherwise, the room will feel out of balance.

Getting Personal

{ "In my mind, there is no better evidence of the divine, or a neutral palette's ability to inspire, than the quiet calm that descends after a snowfall. Every child sees snow as magical and can tell you that no two snowflakes are alike. As an adult, I am still awed by the infinite, intricate designs that will land on my glove, and melt away forever a moment later. I love to snow ski and shushing down a mountain in pure white powder always lifts my spirits. Snow brings me great clarity. I see the world in a fresh, new way. Living with neutrals is a clean and clear feeling." }

ACCENT YOUR ROOM WITH COLOR.
GIVE IT A FACE LIFT AND NEW *personality.*

Give your neutral palette a shot in the arm with a healthy dose of color. You'll find it will lift your spirits and improve your attitude. Remember, a beautiful room will change your life!

Red: A powerful, energizing color associated with passion, excitement and dynamism. Red can warm and enrich any room.

Purple: Most closely associated with royalty, purple is the color of drama and creativity and it creates a rich, powerful space.

Blue: The color of relaxation and tranquility, blue is a universal favorite.

Green: A calming color most strongly associated with nature, green cools and enlarges a space, creating a tranquil and quiet room.

Brown: From dark, traditional mahogany to the lightest casual country pine, brown imparts warmth and can be the perfect background for lively touches in accessories or patterns.

BLUEsky thinking

blues

Think blue, and you might imagine a cool splash in a pool in the heat of summer, laying on your back and gazing in wonder at a star-lit, midnight sky, lines of ink on a page, or the sea before a storm. Think blue a bit longer and you'll find that you may associate the color with spring (the first robin's egg you found as a child?) safety (the policeman who appears at your side in time of need), or even reliability (a navy-blue suit looks stylish and correct on both men and women in nearly every social situation).

While the phrase "feeling blue" describes sadness, blue may also inspire feelings of pride and patriotism (three cheers for the red, white and…), and of course, nearly every-one who thinks blue, thinks of little boys. Some also associate blue with spiritual mat-ters, like peace and heaven. Have you ever noticed that in almost every stained glass window, the Virgin Mary is always portrayed wearing a blue robe?

There's nothing more crisp or classic than the combination of blue and white. It makes me think of blueberries and cream, a favorite china pattern, sails snapping in the wind, and stripes on a wall.

Getting Personal

"Whenever I see blue I think of my son Seth's eyes. He's in heaven now, but God gave me the gift of this wonderful color so that I would remember my child each day when I look up at the sky. Thank you, God, for the color blue! Blue is as peaceful as the sky above, guaranteed to lift your spirits."

BLUE MOOD

Given that blue is so relaxing for body and soul, it is no wonder that it is the most popular color in our stressed-out world. As easy to live with as a well-worn pair of jeans, blue is simply comfortable and familiar. For me, blue represents the sanctuary of the ocean. By painting a wall or an entire room blue and combining shades of brown, you can tap into the colors of sea and sand, two of nature's most soothing elements.

Blue sapphire.

Remember when Princess Diana's blue sapphire engagement ring made the cover of every magazine in the world? It was a modern-day fairytale and every woman I know wanted to try on that gorgeous hunk of jewelry and walk down the aisle with a prince. There is a certain grandeur to deep tones of blue.

Did you know?

Blue's association with sea and sky makes it ideal for opening up small spaces like home offices. Interestingly enough, research has shown that the cooler shades of blue can even make you smarter — people who take tests under ceilings that have been painted a frosty hue reportedly score higher than those taking tests under ceilings painted other colors. Imagine the great work you'll do if you paint your home office ceiling this youthful and contemporary-minded color!

Touches of blue here and there are a calming influence, but too much of a good thing is, well, too much. If it's beginning to look like you've got a serious case of the blues, break up your scheme with a little contrast, as I've done in the photo at left. Green is a natural choice since blue and green are naturally harmonious colors that comfort your soul. (Picture lying in a green field under a blue sky…Mother Nature knew what she was doing!)

Left: Sheraton Sage green walls paired with blue upholstery makes for a comforting mix that's very easy to live with. Harmonic Tan, Artifact and Mossy Gold also add a jazzy note to blue.

See Paint Index, page 133.

Area rugs, like the one above, are an integral part of any well-decorated room today. Given that rugs are not permanent fixtures (you can just roll them up if you move), they are a smart investment for the home and one that is very much in style. Flip through any decorating magazine and you'll find that almost all of the room settings in the photographs feature an area rug on a bare floor. Besides looking fashionable, area rugs are really functional works of art that quell excessive sound while adding warmth and color.

DESIGN TIP

To add interest to an otherwise dull room, paint vertical stripes on the walls, one-foot wide, side by side, in three subtle shade changes. (Just move up one notch, and down one notch from your very favorite blue on a color strip). This technique looks divine with neutral fabrics on a sofa or the top of a bed. For even more visual impact, accent softer shades on the walls with accessories in darker tones.

Red Hot
excitement

brick   warm red   cherry

reds

Call it scarlet, ruby or rouge, crimson, carnation or cherry, claret or cardinal, red by any name is the most exciting color in the spectrum. From earliest times, this dynamic hue has been associated with passion, peril, revolution ("The red coats are coming!"), embarrassment ("Oh, you blush!"), and of course, love ("Kiss me you fool!"). When it comes to decorating, red can warm and enrich any room, making it feel cozier. If red appeals to your daring side, use it in any room where there's plenty of activity, such as a kitchen. If you're a little less adventurous, try it as an accent and finishing touch. After all, wasn't it a young woman in ruby slippers who told us, "There's no place like home?"

Your home is an extension of you, so express your personality. A fabulous red microfiber makes a strong statement and energizes the room at left, while the floral pattern on this page, though still red, is a little more laid-back.

Getting Personal

{ "In 1963 I was named Miss Poinsettia and I've loved red ever since. I feel like this color on the inside, and powerful and in control whenever I wear it. Over the years I've learned that I photograph well in the orange tones of red. I think every woman should be aware of her best colors and fill her closets accordingly! If red is your favorite, do not hesitate to cover your walls with this powerful color. Red looks great with stark white trim paint. So crisp and clean!" }

TRAFFIC-STOPPING, ATTENTION-GETTING RED

Red is a winner

Red has long been associated with danger, from the stop sign at a busy intersection to seeing "red" during an argument, and dynamism (try wearing red to your next important business meeting and you'll see what I mean), but red can also be quite comforting. Imagine a red-flannel shirt, a cheerful red barn in the countryside, or geraniums on Mother's day. Red is a winner, whatever your style!

Days of wine & roses

In the language of flowers, red roses represent passionate love. As the poet Robert Burns once penned, "O my love's like a red, red rose, that's newly sprung in June. O my love's like the melody, that's sweetly played in tune."

Ruby red

"I have a ruby ring that I like to wear. The first real piece of jewelry I ever purchased for myself, it didn't cost much 20 years ago when I bought it to celebrate landing my first big design project. It still makes me feel happy and in control of my life whenever I see it on my finger. Ruby red is a rich and powerful color."

Did you know?

Here's a hint red-lovers should remember when shopping for a sofa or chair. If a sofa's fabric is red, or features a predominantly red pattern like the loveseat pictured on the opposite page, bear in mind that the sofa may look bigger than it actually is after you place it in your room. If your room happens to be exceptionally large and your goal is to make it feel more intimate, match the color on your walls to the red in the sofa fabric. If your room is exceptionally small, don't shy away from red. Just use smaller doses, such as a red mat on a framed picture, or a red ceramic planter as we show here.

The "right" color is the one that suits you. Avocado on the walls plays up the leafy pattern on the loveseat (right), but Roycroft Suede or Golden Fleece work equally well too.

See Paint Index, page 134.

RED, WHITE AND BLUE...

and a touch of green!

Given all that's happened in the past few years, Americans are feeling a new appreciation for all things red, white and blue. In fact, the color combination, and its symbolic association with freedom, says "U.S.A." all over the world. This doesn't mean you have to drape your room in the stars and stripes however. The tri-color combo can be as subtle as it is in the room pictured at left. Here, the primary colors of red and blue add punch to neutral upholstery without being overpowering. The reason this look works is because one color, in this case white, is dominant, and we accented with red and blue. The touch of green adds life and keeps your room from looking like the American flag.

Warm reception

There's nothing quite as warm or inviting as a red door. You might decide to paint your front door red simply because it's charming (and attention-getting!). Then again, many churches paint their doors red to symbolize sanctuary and protection from evil, and the ancient Chinese believed a red door was a sign of luck. Whatever your reason for red, it's sure to add personality to your house, and beckon your friends and family to come in and stay awhile.

DESIGN TIP

My favorite way to decorate a foyer is to introduce your family to all who enter by turning the area into a photo gallery of sorts. Pictures are important and there's nothing more charming than a house filled with memories. To make your displays even more special, try grouping photos by theme. If you have a large family, gather photos of everyone as children at approximately the same age so that you can see the similarities. For example, your grandparents at age ten, your parents at ten, your children at ten, and if appropriate, your grandchildren. Try placing all the married children on the mantel, or all the graduation and school photos on a console table. The idea is to divide by theme so that the display tells a story and to change the displays to suit your mood or the time of year. During Christmas, I show off pictures of my children taken during holidays past. All are framed in (you guessed it) red!

GOLDEN
opportunities

yellows

Let the sunshine in! "Yellow Submarine." "Goodbye Yellow Brick Road." "Here Comes the Sun." Like a happy canary, yellow simply sings with cheerfulness, brightening our day and inviting us to tap our feet and hum along. As lovely as a summer's day, yellow is the spirit-lifter, the sunny center of our universe, and a universal sign of hope that a brand new day is on the way. We even tie yellow ribbons around old oak trees to show our support of troops or missing loved ones who are far from home.

As one of the primary hues, yellow, like red, grabs our attention (there's a reason for all those yellow highlighters in the office!), and won't let go. We don't mind. Like Dorothy skipping down her famous brick path, or moths to the proverbial flame, we happily follow yellow wherever it leads. "Good Day Sunshine!"

Check out this lovely example of a golden opportunity. The living room at left just exudes positive energy. Don't you want to stay awhile? Starlight, star bright, the first star I see tonight is…yellow!

Getting Personal

"Daisies got their name from the Old English phrase 'day's eye,' because the flower opens to the sun in the morning. Associated with youthful beauty and cheerfulness, my son called daisies 'happy flowers.' Fill your room with happiness, whether real or silk. Daisies will definitely put a smile on your face and add life to a space. Fresh and clean, daisies help spread tiny touches of yellow throughout a room."

BLONDES
HAVE MORE FUN...
OR DO THEY?

Ever since Rapunzel let down her golden hair for her prince to climb (ouch!), I've been fascinated by flaxen tresses. Fairy-tale princesses aside, some of the most famous blondes aren't really blonde at all. Marilyn Monroe was really a redhead and Hollywood legend has it that Lana Turner bleached her hair so much it actually fell out! I was born a redhead (more like an orange head that faded to strawberry blonde), but I have chosen to live this side of life as a blonde…and I'm definitely having a lot of fun!

When choosing paints…

It's a good idea to stick to the sunnier side of yellow, whether lemon, citrine, canary, corn, flax, sunflower, primrose, butter or even yolk. Think twice before splashing on yellows with greenish casts, especially in rooms where you spend a lot of time, no matter how much you love the shade. The reflected light from yellow-greens can make your skin tone appear sallow or jaundiced. (Yikes!) Golden colors are comfortable and compelling when chosen correctly.

61

Did you know?

Since yellow stimulates the mind, use it with abandon in the living room, dining room, kitchen or home office. Lean toward creamier shades in a bedroom however, so you'll be sure to get enough rest. While yellow is generally characterized as a mood lifter, especially in those who can't get outside as often as they might like, some researchers say it may actually make babies and small children feel anxious. This is something to consider before you paint the nursery. The key to decorating for a happy baby is soft butter tones on the walls with accents of pink or blue as appropriate!

Baguette on the walls combined with beige upholstery makes for a sophisticated honey of a look. For a jolt of something different, try accents of Latte, Cardboard or Java.

See Paint Index, page 134.

Details count

Decorative accessories represent a golden opportunity for those who are still a little shy about experimenting with color. Here, honeyed wood pieces add warmth, while the black accents bring drama to the space. Remember to use black sparingly and sprinkle it throughout the room.

DESIGN TIP

Try massing accessories together to tell a story. Just be sure that your collections don't equal clutter, because clutter distracts the eye, disquiets the soul and makes cleaning more arduous. Use odd numbers of three to five items in a group for impact, as we've done on the coffee table at right. When using a pair of something, such as matching candlesticks, add a glass bowl or an interesting box, for example, to complete your grouping and add visual interest.

PURPLE
passion

| eggplant | grape | dusk |

purples

Whether violet or magenta, eggplant or thistle, purple is the color most closely associated with royalty, drama, creativity and spirituality. Deep purples like blackberry and plum are often associated with riches (think jewels), while lighter, more ladylike tones like lavender and violet speak of old-fashioned romance. Since purple results from combining a warm color (red) with a cool color (blue), you can heat up or cool down your décor depending on the shade you choose. The redder the purple, the hotter the look, and the bluer the purple, well, you get the picture. May visions of sugar plums dance in your head!

Since how I feel in my studio space is so important to me, I've been known to paper a wall purple because the color is believed to stimulate imagination and creativity.

Getting Personal

{ "There is a certain mystical or spiritual quality attached to purple. A child of the '60s, I remember well the psychedelic scene and the 'hippie' types who wore it (I was one of them!). I still haven't gotten over the comfort and power of wearing purple and I still love those Bohemian styles. Beware, purple walls are dramatic and bold, not for the timid in spirit." }

IN PRAISE OF GRAPES

Lavender blue dilly dilly

In the language of flowers, purple statice stands for remembrance and lasting beauty. Since it's the only flower that retains its original color as it dries, I always use purple statice liberally in arrangements. I think it is the one flower capable of bringing the brilliance of summer into the gray of winter. And, it is the one flower that remains as a memento of your special occasion. Lavender, however, is my personal purple favorite, probably because I associate the flower with my travels to France. (Provence is the lavender capital of the world, and there's nothing as lovely to me as the fields of purple and green set against the sun-baked hillsides). For centuries, lavender has been used to promote sleep and relaxation. I like to mist my sheets with a lavender-infused spray. It's dreamy! There's also nothing like taking a bath with a bar of lavender soap. Paint a room in the soft colors of lavender and let the relaxation and tranquility transform your state of mind!

Did you know?

Long associated with artistic impulses, painters, composers and writers often surround themselves with purple. Supposedly, Leonardo DaVinci felt that violet light, such as that which would stream through the stained glass window of a church, exponentially increased meditative powers. Pick up a paint brush and get started. You may ignite an undiscovered talent waiting to surface!

Contemporary looks plum divine with walls painted in Flexible Gray. Try Bunglehouse Gray and Crewel Tan as hip accents.

See Paint Index, page 135.

rresting amethyst

My favorite possession is an amethyst pendant I purchased in the estate area of a jewelry store. I love that someone else owned it before me and I often wonder what her life was like. Amethysts were reportedly a favorite of Catherine the Great and Egyptian royals, and figure prominently in Britain's collection of Crown Jewels. DaVinci wrote that the stone could dispel evil thoughts and the stone was a symbol of piety in the Catholic Church. Even today, Catholic bishops often wear amethyst rings.

DESIGN TIP

Color is the key to integrating different periods and styles of furniture. Take a look at the decorative accessories pictured at left, for example. The companion prints pick up the purple in the glass vase and the blossoms in the flower arrangement. To check if the accent color you've chosen is carried throughout your room in a cohesive way, stand in the middle of your room and turn slowly in a complete circle. Is there color on the floor in the form of an area rug? Is the same color represented on the furniture in a throw or decorative pillow, or on the tabletops? Does it carry over to the wall décor?

GREEN with envy

greens

Green is a calming color that speaks of nature and life. For this reason, green is almost always viewed as a positive color...unless you are green with envy of course! Green is also friendly. It seems to get along with every shade it's paired with. Just look at your garden. Inside, green is often used to cool and enlarge a space. Indeed, hospitals everywhere use it to create tranquil environments that promote healing. Even if green is not your favorite color, and you wouldn't like to live in a room done entirely in green, do add greenery to your décor to give your room (whatever the color) life. Not to worry if your thumb is less than green. Silk arrangements work just as well without any of the fuss! Can you tell that the greenery shown in the photo at left is silk? Gotcha!

In nature, green is partnered with every hue imaginable.

Getting Personal

{ Remember sour apple gum? As a child it was one of my favorites! Today I'm a pie-baker thanks to my mother, Phyllis. She taught me how to bake the finest pie on the church dessert table. There's nothing like the first bite of a Granny Smith apple. Whether you accent your room with fresh green apples or faux, they will bring the same kind of flavor to your decor! }

GREEN IS
SPRING GRASS AND
CHRISTMAS PINE

The color green

Lovers of historical romance know that courtesans would bite into tangy green limes to redden their lips.
(Modern lipstick is a lot less messy!)

Enchanting emeralds

Highly valued as a gemstone, emeralds are said to drive away evil spirits and
protect the virtue of the wearer. Historically speaking, a gift of emerald jewelry to a young woman was, shall we say, a protective measure. Still a favorite
of many women, wearing emeralds near your face will bring out the green
in your hazel eyes, make baby blues appear even bluer, and bring out the
best in brown-eyed girls. Thus, a perfect color for a room to look beautiful in!

Did you know?

If you're designing a room for a man in your life, you generally can't go wrong with hunter green. Whether it's the call of nature and the great outdoors, or something that instinctively harkens back to the Garden of Eden, men seem to gravitate to green. Use it liberally in a den or family room or as an excellent choice for your husband's study.

Walls painted in Artifact have a calming influence on the elegant scene at right. For more drama, try Leatherbound, or Ivoire for a super sophisticated look.

See Paint Index, page 135.

Elements of design

Architectural elements in a room are like a fashion model's good bone structure. Decorative windows, mouldings, columns, ceiling medallions and wainscoting bring charm and interest to a space. Once made only of plaster and wood, these elements of design are available today in plastics that can be painted or stained. Check out your local home builder store and add a few details to enhance your room.

DESIGN TIP

Remember the days when your mother was passionate about having draperies on decorative rods because it was such the fashion? Well, times have changed and heavy drapes have gone the way of wall-to-wall carpeting. Like bare wood floors covered in the occasional area rug, the trend today is toward less-fussy, less-dressed interiors and this includes windows. Plantation-style blinds are functional and make for a streamlined look, but if that's a little stark for your personal taste, try adding a decorative rod with a sheer scarf that ties into the colors of your room for an open and airy effect.

Earthly elements

earth

From the flaming oranges and crimsons of falling autumn leaves to the ginger goodness of homemade pumpkin pie, when it comes to decorating, spicy colors like cinnamon, nutmeg and squash are like comfort food for the soul. In fact, the color orange is actually said to encourage appetite, so it's a fine choice for a dining room. Of course, you can count on the of-the-earth shades in this classic color family to look simply scrumptious wherever you choose to use them. The room at left is a great example of rich rust colors used predominantly on the walls. This room feels warm and cozy even though it is quite large and spacious. The oversized sofa contributes to the warmth of the room and the pillow design adds interest.

Like the hot fudge on a dish of vanilla ice cream, brown makes everything extra delicious.

Getting Personal

{ "I am a chocoholic...have been for years. The smell of chocolate drives me wild. (I blame Mr. Hershey for the extra ten pounds I constantly fight.) I love to wear the color brown. It makes me feel safe and comfortable. When used in home décor, I interpret brown as down-to-earth, cozy and secure. It is an easy color to live with and one that welcomes you home each night." }

Western style

Earthy colors have long been associated with Southwestern style. You can kick up your decorating flavor a notch or two with orange, adobe, terra cotta or clay on the walls. You're only a paint can away from the red rocks of Sedona, or the serenity of sun-baked Scottsdale. Add energy to your room today.

Did you know?

Since brown tones can be found in nearly every home's wood furniture finishes, browns can be used in almost any room. For this reason, it's among the safest bets for those who are a little shy about experimenting with color. A brown-red adds personality to the fabulous room at right.

Rookwood Red makes this space feel comfy and secure. If you're after something less spicy, try Baguette or Aurora Brown on the walls, or as accent colors.

See Paint Index, page 135.

Walk on the wild side

Animal prints have long been a favorite of both men and women, from the clothing we wear to the furniture we decorate with, even as accents in the cars we drive. I think skin prints and patterns tap into our primal nature and make us all feel a little sexier. If you're looking to tap the wilder side of earth's elements and transport yourself to another part of the world, paint a wall a rusty red and then add an animal print to the room. The results will make you purr!

$\mathcal{C}$hocolate

Brown paint on the walls was once considered a no-no, but is now very chic. You'll find that choco-late or cocoa colors with hints of red make for a very sophisticated room. Choose a medium shade of brown with neutral furniture in a small room for a cozy feeling, and remember that there's noth-ing like the combination of brown and white. Can we ever forget Julia Roberts in "Pretty Woman?" The brown and white polka-dot dress she wore to the polo match was so charming and fresh! In the same way, the room above invites you to come in and stay awhile. Ah, the comfort of chocolate and white cocoa!

DESIGN TIP

Given that rug patterns are often bold and complex, they will instantly jazz up a room with neutral or plain-patterned upholstery. For this reason, rugs do wonders for leather sofas. On the other hand, if you have a sofa full of personality and pattern, take a back or seat cushion with you as you shop for a rug. If the rug you like is displayed on a hanging rack in the store, make sure you lower the rug to the floor, then take a step back so you can see the actual effect of your sofa pattern with the rug.

BLACK
magic

black

Black lacks brightness and absorbs all light. And over the years that's given black a bad rap. Indeed, black has long been associated with magic and mystery, evil and even death. As sober as it can be, black can also be sexy, glamorous and the height of sophistication. When decorating, it's best to use black judiciously, so you don't end up with a room that feels overly dark or depressing! The other caveat to remember is that while solid black fabrics and carpeting won't show dirt as quickly, lint and light-colored pet hair will really stand-out. The room setting at left is a perfect example of black used successfully.

Black is the color of my true love's hair...truly!

Getting Personal

{ "I wear mostly black, drive a black car, and have a black leather sofa. I am comfortable in black and it will always be my first choice. A look into my closet will quickly tell you that black is my favorite color to wear. And a look at my living room, my favorite color to accent with. Never fear you lovers of black, you will always be in style, no matter the year!" }

BLACK IS
STYLISH, TIMELESS AND EVER-POPULAR

A little black dress

A black dress is a staple in any woman's closet. Some (like me) have more than one! Every girl knows there's nothing like taking a cocktail-party staple like a little black dress and adding accent colors of silver, gold and red to take a look from minimalist to magnificent. Rooms are no different. The most common use of black in living rooms is black leather upholstery. To mix it up a bit, add personality and excitement, use basic primary colors in accents (such as red pillows or a red and black geometric rug). Remember black is always appropriate and a safe bet!

Earn your stripes

Looking to add an element of excitement or exoticism to a room dominated by black? Whether your style is West Indies, Ethnic, out of Africa or eclectic, you can't go wrong with a black-and-white animal print accent. Hunt for something in a zebra print, whether a rug, throw or pillows. Then settle down with your favorite Hemingway novel and prepare to be transported!

Did you know?

Want your house to stand out on the block? When it comes to curb appeal, nothing speaks louder than black shutters and a black door, whether your house is painted khaki, sage green or white. It's a powerful look that makes a statement about the people who live within!

Black tie-affair

Leather has long been viewed as a luxurious option for car interiors and clothing. When it comes to home furnishings, leather has become a passion for those who seek high fashion, style and durability. Leather has a certain sexiness that appeals to both men and women. In the picture to the right, we dressed up a comfy looking sofa with great-looking tables in a merlot finish, a contemporary area rug, updated black-and-white framed artwork and spiffy lamps. The black leather grouping on its own could be viewed as boxy and overwhelming for the room. The rug and accessories are essential to ground this much black and soften its appeal.

ADD A JOLT OF COLOR FOR SOMETHING dIFFerEnT.

When it comes to classic color combinations, black-and-white tops the always-in-style charts. Yet, as cool and crisp as black-and-white feels at first glance, pure black and white can begin to seem downright cold and boring over time. Adding another color, even in small doses, makes this classic pairing easier to live with in the long term.

Black with RED accents!

Black with PURPLE accents!

Black with BLUE accents!

DESIGN TIP

If you're an animal lover, you may not love the effect pets can have on your furniture. Here's a quick tip for anyone who has a cat that has used a sofa arm for a clawing post. Remember the razor with the flat blades that your father used? Put in a new blade, but don't tighten it all the way. (Be careful!) With a very gentle touch, lightly swipe it over the effected area to remove any frayed threads and de-fuzz the fabric. Then, casually toss a good-looking throw over the arm as a visual distraction from the damage. If the sofa is in such bad shape that this fix won't fool anybody, think about investing in a slipcover.

Pretty in pink

pinks

Emotionally soothing and romantic, pink is the color of "positivity" and puppy love. A natural sedative, pink is particularly right for the bedroom, nursery or bath. Anywhere, in fact, where the emphasis is on peace and quiet. Pink often signifies romance and has a positive impact on the emotions of the heart. Like purple, pink is a mixture, a union of red and white, and therefore pink blends passion with purity. Pale pinks represent the sweetness of youth, while vibrant pinks are high-spirited and express energy. Pink is light, fun and playful…think pink lemonade, pink champagne and pink grapefruit!

In some cases pink is for girls, but I always look twice at a man who is secure enough to wear a pink polo shirt or designer tie.

Getting Personal

"I feel sexy in pink, whether I'm wearing pink lipstick, a pink sweater or sipping a pink drink. As girly as it is, however, pink is as powerful as red when it comes to making a statement about femininity and strength. And, thanks to breast cancer research, pink ribbons have become a universal symbol of caring and concern. Nothing gave me greater pleasure than raising money for the City of Hope Cancer Center in honor of my friend, Annie, a breast cancer survivor."

THINK PINK

Pink gets your attention with a whisper

Pink adds a level of femininity to a room without going overboard. We don't have to be Elle Woods in "Legally Blonde" to make the most of the color. Walk on the softer side of your personality…try pink for a sweet change!

Cherry blossom

Pink is uplifting. In the South, pink azaleas herald spring, and millions travel to our nation's capital every April to take in the showy pink cherry blossoms in bloom along the Potomac. (A sight so lovely to behold we even celebrate it with a parade!) Clearly, our souls crave the sense of change the seasons bring. Decorating with pink helps us translate the same sense of freshness and renewal into our home. A sense of new life is added to a room whenever we add pink.

Did you know?

Pink is warm and flattering and imparts a healthy glow to most skin tones, which is the reason many women opt to use light bulbs that have been tinted pink. If you're looking to be seen in your best light, try accenting your pink color scheme with burgundy, gray and cream for drama. You're ready for your close-up now!

Innocence on the walls leaves this room tickled pink. Try Glamour and Abalone Shell either as the wall color or as accents.

See Paint Index, page 136.

The icing on the cake

Decorative accents like framed art finish off a room like icing on a, well you know. But if the budget is tight and your walls are looking bare, pick up a paintbrush and get creative. Here's a contemporary-minded example: Paint three walls of the room dove gray, and since we're thinking pink, add a one-foot wide, horizontal stripe in blush at eye level, to all three of the walls. Then, paint the fourth wall entirely in blush. This technique, which works equally well with other color combinations, eliminates the need to purchase artwork. (Actually, everyone will be asking for the name of your artist!)

DESIGN TIP

Bear in mind that lighting affects color, so when shopping for furnishings, it's usually a good idea to view your area rug and upholstery choices in a situation that approximates the lighting you'll use in your room. People often make the mistake of feeling that they have to view their upholstery fabric in natural light. This is something that I have never understood. Your sofa is not going to sit on the lawn; it's going to sit in a room that has entirely different lighting. Be careful not to make this mistake. It's best to check out a sofa cushion from your local store, and bring it home to view it in the actual room setting, alongside floor, wall and window coverings. If you're completely redecorating, don't forget to bring all your paint, carpet and fabric samples into the room so that you can see the total effect in the right light.

AFTERWORD
AFTERWORD
AFTERWORD
AFTERWORD
AFTERWORD
AFTERWORD
AFTERWORD
AFTERWORD

afterword

O.k., now that we've completed our journey through color, I hope I am leaving you with a sense of confidence and empowerment.

This book was created to give you a comfort level with color. Now, that we've overcome your fears of making a decorating color mistake, the next step will be to make changes more often, maybe even as often as you change your wardrobe with the seasons.

Like many women, I'm drawn to the latest colors in fashion each spring and fall. In the same way that our mothers were attracted to turquoise in the '60s, and avocado green and harvest gold for their kitchens in the '70s, our research has shown that women today also want the latest fashion colors for their interiors. It is important to understand that color trends always start in apparel and then work forward into home. I'll be exploring the intimate connection between apparel and home fashions in one of my next books, *Coming Out of the Closet*. Watch for it! In the meantime, remember that a bucket of paint is the quickest way to translate fashion's hottest new directions into your home's decor without breaking the budget.

Lastly, I want to hear how a beautiful room has changed your life. Send your stories to designteam@conniepost.com and let us know if we can share them with others.

Questions commonly Asked

Question: I'm not bad looking and I don't smell. Why is that every time I bring a date back to my apartment I never see her again? Women seem to take one look at my place and run. Any ideas?

Answer: Like most guys, you probably bought new clothes, moussed your hair, applied cologne, washed your car and wined and dined her. But you forgot one crucial thing. Your home is a reflection of your true self, and the way you choose to furnish it is perhaps one of the most personal and revealing statements you can make about yourself. This means you have to spend just as much time and effort on packaging your place as you do on packaging you. In fact, a recent survey found that 80 percent of singles are checking out home décor to determine a date's future potential. The same survey found that 37 percent have actually fled the scene and cut a hot date short because of "scary" décor.

So look around your main living space. How "scary" is it? Can you honestly say it reflects the real you? Compare your room to your car. Is it as sexy and as cool? Is it clean and as well maintained? If not, your first move should be to de-clutter and clean up the area. Then take stock. Is storage a problem? Are there piles of magazines and newspapers, and CDs? Are you staring at a wall of black boxes with enough wire to launch the space shuttle? If so, your next move should be to purchase bookshelves, an armoire or an entertainment center with cabinets to hide all the mess.

After getting the space in order, you can think about the design of your bachelor pad. I suggest that you focus on finding a really nice, comfortable sofa (after all, it's the first place she's most likely to sit down). Then paint your walls a fun color that coordinates with the sofa and add a simple piece of artwork that you think reflects who you are. (Incidentally, if you choose to hang a picture of a woman, please make sure she's fully clothed). None of this should sound remotely daunting, but if you're the least bit uneasy about coordinating color and style, just ask a female salesperson for a little free advice. (Who knows? She could turn out to be the one you've been looking for all along!)

Question: My new in-laws are visiting our home for the first time and I'm nervous. How can I make a good first impression?

Answer: Concentrate on your foyer! Technically speaking, this is the area just inside your front door, and it's the first impression that every visitor has of your home. In terms of design, the foyer is generally a good spot to splurge on upscale accoutrements because the space is usually small. (This means the addition of tile or marble to the floor, or a beautiful area rug for color and pattern is doable on limited budgets). Think about the way you use the space. Do you need a furniture piece for storage, or a table to lay down your keys and bring in the mail? How about a mirror to check your look on the way out or before opening the door? My favorite way to decorate a foyer is to introduce your family to all who enter by turning the area into a photo gallery of sorts. Just choose your favorite shots, frame and display. It's a charming way to celebrate those you love.

Question: All the decorating magazines are great, but I've never seen any address my problem. My husband collects small model cars and he has so many our family room looks like Daytona. I can't complain, because my thing is frogs and what started out as a cute theme for the bathroom is threatening to overrun the house. Any ideas?

Answer: First of all, relax. Unless dreams of Kermit running laps around the living room are keeping you awake at night, you're perfectly normal. We're all collectors of one odd thing or another. My passion happens to be pop-up books. The only difference is that books are easy enough to corral. Yet, frogs and model cars really aren't all that difficult to deal with. Just practice the following mantra: Every woman needs a curio cabinet! Curio cabinets are the answer for all the emotional buying of things that don't necessarily work with our décor. Most so-called design experts advocate moving these things out of view (or out the door altogether), but that's not realistic. A curio cabinet allows you to clean up your act, control clutter and showcase your special things behind glass in an attractive, organized manner. Rather than hiding your collections, a curio makes them the focal point and conversation piece in your room. Added benefit? Curios cut down on the need for endless dusting!

Question: We've just moved into a great new home, complete with a "great" room, which includes the kitchen, a space for eating and a larger space with a fireplace. Now that all the excitement of the move has worn off, I'm over-whelmed and at a loss for how to make all this "great" space feel like home.

Answer: Don't let that big empty space make you feel small for even a minute. As a designer, I'm a big fan of space, but I'll admit that over-sized rooms with few walls can be just as tricky to decorate as the too-small variety. The key to taming a large room, like any big problem, is to mentally break it down into three, smaller pieces. Think of it as one part media (include your TV in this section along with the electronics), one part entertainment (a card or game table, computer station maybe?), and one part conversation area. Once you've defined the three sections, arrange your furnishings according to function and your great room will begin to feel great in no time. Incidentally, this three-part formula also works wonders on studio apartments and college dorm rooms!

Question: I don't have a big budget, but I really want to re-do my master bedroom. I know I can't afford to buy everything I want at once and I'll probably need to attack the project in stages. Is there a right or wrong place to start?

Answer: First, bear in mind that with the favorable interest rates today, it's common practice for furniture retailers to offer financing options that often don't require payments for an extended period of time. So, it may be that you can afford more than you think you can, and depending on what you've got in mind, you might be surprised to find that you can, indeed, have the bedroom of your dreams right now. But let's just say that you have to go slow and stick to a plan. When it comes to re-doing a bedroom, the two most important style statements are the bed itself, and the dresser. Since the bed is by far the most important element, I'd start there.

Although bedrooms are typically sold in suites (pronounced suit, not sweet, which is only important if you want to impress your local furniture salesperson), most retailers will allow you to buy individual pieces of a collection if you're not ready for an entire roomful at once. Plus, some of the most popular looks today are more eclectic in nature—meaning that you're free to express yourself and not every piece in your room has to match.

But back to the bed…step one is to find a headboard and footboard that you absolutely love because the bed will set the style and tone of your room overall. Step two is to outfit that bed with a fabulous mattress. Before you balk (I'm a designer so I can relate to the idea that you're more interested in "pretty" at the moment), we need to talk about the function of a bedroom. Bottom line, your bedroom is for sleeping, and a good mattress is the foundation of a good night's sleep. (And trust me, when you sleep well, no matter how you've decorated the room, everything looks better in the morning.) So squeeze the most you can out of your budget and invest it in the best mattress set you can afford. Take it from a working Mom…it will be the one decorating decision you'll never regret.

After you're as comfy as the princess before the pea was placed, turn to the second most important piece of furniture in the bedroom: the dresser. If your budget is really limited, think about buying the dresser base and forgoing the mirror for the moment. You can always dress up a mirror you already have with paint in the accent color of your choice and make do until your ready for the next round.

Now, here's the key to making this work: Before you purchase anything, have a frank discussion with your salesperson. You need to know how long you can expect the store to carry the group you are interested in. In other words, if you're purchasing in stages, and eventually want to add other pieces in a given collection, you don't want a closeout, or something from a clearance center! Of course, if a sale price is just too tempting and a year later you find you are part owner of a discontinued line, it's still not the end of the world. You can always add accent furniture pieces in different colors, a painted armoire for example, or a pair of interesting night tables, skirted in a fabric that coordinates with your bed linens.

As for finishing touches, the bedroom is the one place to use color that pleases you, so paint with abandon. (If your bedroom is small, try painting just the wall behind the bed to make the bed the center of attention, and then carry the color through the room with decorative pieces and linens, and maybe an area rug that will feel good under your bare feet in the morning). Finally, plantation blinds are a quick fix for window treatments when budgets are tight, and you can pick up good-looking, inexpensive versions at your local home center. Sleep tight!

Question: The company that I work for recently downsized and I'm thinking about starting a home business so I can be there when my children come home from school. I'd like to convert my formal dining room into a home office, but I'm worried about what people might think. Any suggestions?

Answer: You're not the first person who has asked me this question. The formal dining room is often a fairly secluded space within the layout of a home, and with our modern lifestyles, often sits unused for months on end. Families congregate in the kitchen or great room for meals while the dining room table collects dust or acts as a catch-all for piles of mail, forgotten home assignments and Little Susie's latest craft project.

If this sounds like the scene at your place, it makes all the sense in the world to put the room to better use. And for working moms, a centrally located space (as dining rooms tend to be) is ideal for those times when you need to finish a project while keeping an eye on your children. So forget what anybody else says. For once, it's all about you!

The key to making it work is to outfit the space with pieces that can serve multiple purposes and still look as though they belong in a home and not in an office building. Furniture stores today have whole departments devoted to the category, and you'll find a wide range of bookcases and desks with hutches to help keep you organized. But try to think beyond the usual desk and chair. A drop-leaf table, for example, can be pushed up against one wall and used as a console to display pictures of the kids. When you need to entertain, move it away from the wall, open it up and go to town. It can also serve as a conference table should that new business of yours take off (as we know it will!).

If your work style is not the neatest, consider adding some louver doors to the space so that you can close the area off in a flash. Company coming? No need to clear the decks. Just shut the doors. Louver doors like the kind used for closets are easily purchased from your local home center and are just as easy to install.

The only caveat is to personalize your workspace and make it an extension of you, just as you would any other room in your home. Along with the family pictures, accessorize with floral arrangements or greenery to add life, and ditch the ubiquitous metal task lighting for a beautiful, residential style lamp to give your office a homey feel. What are you waiting for? It's time to get to work!

Question: I'd like to paint my living room a new and fabulous color and I'm seeing pink everywhere this season. My husband says pink is just for little girls' rooms. Am I crazy to want pink in an area geared for adults? For that matter, if I do manage to make him think pink, will it look passé by the fall?

Answer: You go girl! In a recent survey we conducted in 10 cities about what women want from their furniture buying experience, the vast majority wanted to know about the latest, most fashionable colors to update their homes. So your question is right on, and so are your instincts about color. In fashion speak, pink is the new rose (or the new mauve). We've just come off two years of red and we're ready for something softer, lighter and airier. Bottom line? Pink is very, very current.

Actually, I get questions like yours quite often, which is surprising since homes across America tend to be awash in a sea of off-white. I don't know what everyone is so afraid of. After all, a can of paint is the least expensive way to change the mood of a room. If you really can't live with the results, you're only another paint can away from perfection and a color you adore.

If you're a truly trendy type, and just have to be on fashion's cutting edge at all times, the only caveat to bear in mind when choosing a paint color is that you probably will have to re-paint your room approximately every 18 months since that's the average lifespan of a color in the fashion world. Beware all you budding fashionistas: trend forecasters see tangerine coming on strong. In other words, if your husband is having a problem with pink, imagine what he'll say about citrus!

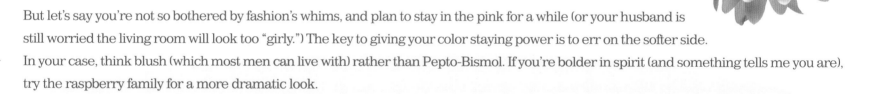

But let's say you're not so bothered by fashion's whims, and plan to stay in the pink for a while (or your husband is still worried the living room will look too "girly.") The key to giving your color staying power is to err on the softer side. In your case, think blush (which most men can live with) rather than Pepto-Bismol. If you're bolder in spirit (and something tells me you are), try the raspberry family for a more dramatic look.

If there was ever a color that makes people happy, pink is it. In fact, pink's "positivity" probably has a lot to do with why we're seeing it in every catalog, magazine and store right now. Events of the past two years mean there are still a lot of depressed people out there and pink helps us look at the bright side whether we're dressed in a pink sweater, carrying a pink jelly bag, or putting on pink lipstick. So paint with abandon.

Pink is also a very transitional color…meaning that it works just as well in a traditional setting as it does in something more contemporary. It pairs well with brown, beige and taupe (your husband will be thrilled!), gray, green and blue. The key to making it work is to carry through the wall color with decorative accents, say, pink throw pillows on a blue sofa, or pink silk flowers in a vase on a table to pull the look together. So plan a date-night with your husband, order a pizza and pick up a brush. I promise you'll be tickled pink with the results!

Question: I recently painted my living room and bought a great-looking sofa, but the room still seems stark. I love art and know I need to hang a picture or two, but I don't want to choose the wrong thing. Are there any rules of thumb?

Answer: Henry James once said, "It is art that makes life," and, when it comes to interior design, nothing adds warmth and beauty to a home like a wonderful, framed piece, so you're on the right track. When decorating with framed art, the most important thing to remember is choose what appeals to you. While it's a good idea to pick a picture featuring colors that complement your sofa fabric, the fact is that art usually outlasts every other element in our decorating schemes. You'll redecorate sooner or later, but most of us never part with the portrait of Mama, the black-and-whites our significant other shot in college, or the little framed print we bought with our husband for our first apartment.

Don't waste time fretting if the Old Master was left to "that" side of the family either, because there are wonderful offerings of wall décor for all tastes (and pocketbooks) available. Since the emphasis in most stores is on good value, it's not expensive at all to create an ever-changing gallery that will keep your home always looking up-to-date and in style.

Framed pictures really act as "glue" in a room—bringing all the different elements together for a cohesive look. Generally speaking, vertical arrangements will make the walls seem taller, while horizontal displays add width to a room. When decorating with more than one piece of art, it's important that all your frames coordinate in some way. In other words, if the large picture over your sofa is framed in gold, don't a hang another framed in silver on the same wall.

Once you've chosen a picture you love in an appropriate frame, follow the six/twelve rule when you're ready to hang it. That is, no picture should ever be closer to the top of the back of your sofa than six inches, and no further away than 12 inches. Higher than a foot, and you'll find you have a disproportionate amount of space between the sofa and your frame. Your picture will appear to be floating off in space.

To ensure placement is just right, lay your picture on the floor in front of your sofa, on top of a sheet of plain newsprint. Trace the shape of the frame on the paper and then cut the newsprint to size. With just a few pieces of tape you can "hang" the paper on your wall, and shift it around to find your picture's ideal spot, without making any unnecessary holes.

Sources and Supplies

FURNITURE
AND DECORATIVE ACCESSORIES
PROVIDED BY
THE FOLLOWING RETAILERS

FINGERS FURNITURE

Houston, Texas

www.fingerfurniture.com

pages: 24, 27, 46, 63, 68, 70, 78, 83, 88

NEBRASKA FURNITURE MART

Omaha, Nebraska and Kansas City, Missouri

www.nebraskafurnituremart.com

pages: 28, 29, 30, 91, 96, 110

ROOMFUL EXPRESS

Pittsburgh, Pennsylvania

www.roomfulexpress.com

pages: 36, 40, 42, 51, 52, 58, 64, 73, 84, 93, 94, 95, 114

PAINT INDEX

This paint index is a handy tool for anyone interested in creating a beautiful room that will change your life. Each room featured in this book has been painted with Sherwin-Williams colors and we have carefully selected companion colors that coordinate with each of the room settings.

Here's how to use it. Find the page with the room you love most, and you'll note that we have given you a number of different colors to choose from, either as accents or as options for the wall color. If your room is large, you may need more intense color for a more dramatic look or to make your room feel cozier. Likewise, if you have a small room, you might choose lighter colors to make your room feel larger. All in all, this index is a quick and easy guide for personalizing your space.

Remember, you're only a bucket of paint away from a whole new you. And, if you don't like the result, you're only another bucket of paint away from perfect happiness. So grab a brush and experiment. Be bold and go for something different.

ROOM SETTINGS: MAIN WALL COLORS AND ACCENTS

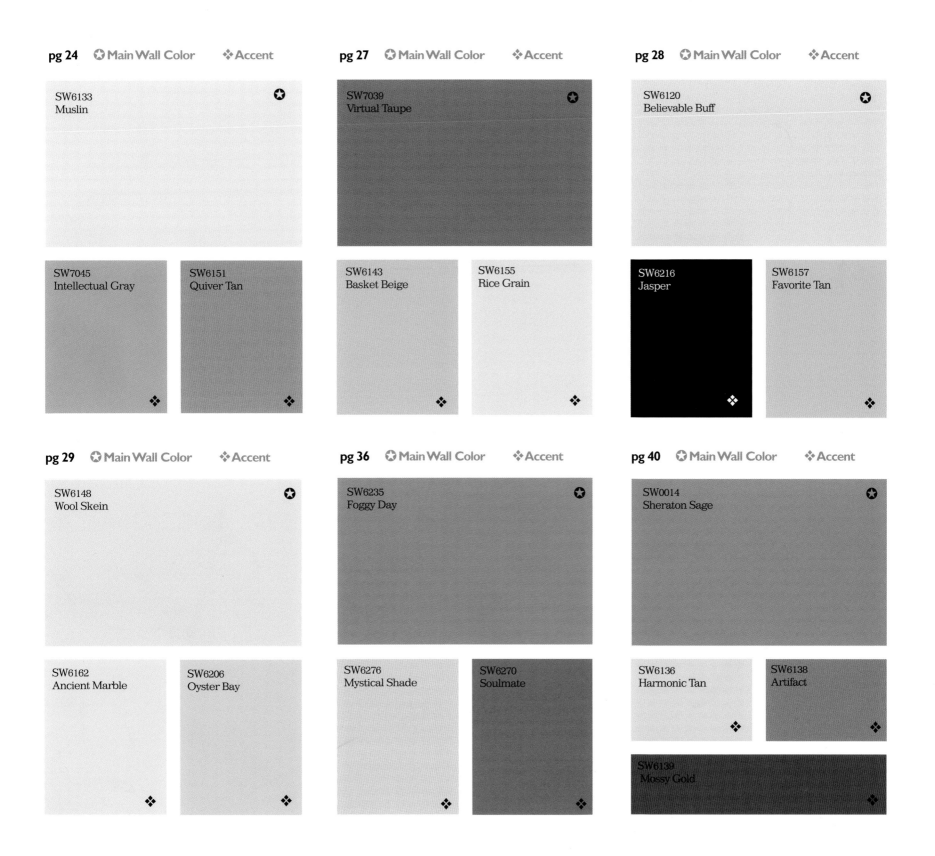

pg 24 ✪ Main Wall Color ❖ Accent

SW6133
Muslin ✪

SW7045
Intellectual Gray ❖

SW6151
Quiver Tan ❖

pg 27 ✪ Main Wall Color ❖ Accent

SW7039
Virtual Taupe ✪

SW6143
Basket Beige ❖

SW6155
Rice Grain ❖

pg 28 ✪ Main Wall Color ❖ Accent

SW6120
Believable Buff ✪

SW6216
Jasper ❖

SW6157
Favorite Tan ❖

pg 29 ✪ Main Wall Color ❖ Accent

SW6148
Wool Skein ✪

SW6162
Ancient Marble ❖

SW6206
Oyster Bay ❖

pg 36 ✪ Main Wall Color ❖ Accent

SW6235
Foggy Day ✪

SW6276
Mystical Shade ❖

SW6270
Soulmate ❖

pg 40 ✪ Main Wall Color ❖ Accent

SW0014
Sheraton Sage ✪

SW6136
Harmonic Tan ❖

SW6138
Artifact ❖

SW6139
Mossy Gold ❖

Colors may shift during the printing process. Please check your local paint store for actual color chips.

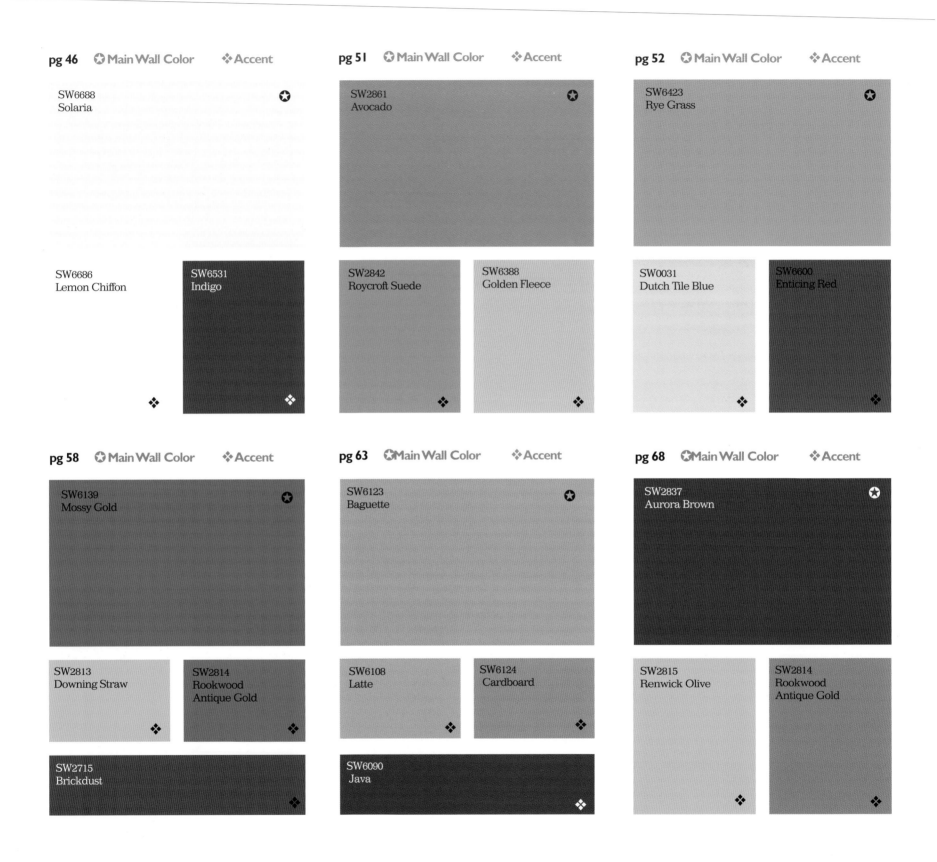

pg 46 ⊕ Main Wall Color ❖ Accent

SW6688
Solaria

SW6686
Lemon Chiffon

SW6531
Indigo

pg 51 ⊕ Main Wall Color ❖ Accent

SW2861
Avocado

SW2842
Roycroft Suede

SW6388
Golden Fleece

pg 52 ⊕ Main Wall Color ❖ Accent

SW6423
Rye Grass

SW0031
Dutch Tile Blue

SW6600
Enticing Red

pg 58 ⊕ Main Wall Color ❖ Accent

SW6139
Mossy Gold

SW2813
Downing Straw

SW2814
Rookwood
Antique Gold

SW2715
Brickdust

pg 63 ⊕ Main Wall Color ❖ Accent

SW6123
Baguette

SW6108
Latte

SW6124
Cardboard

SW6090
Java

pg 68 ⊕ Main Wall Color ❖ Accent

SW2837
Aurora Brown

SW2815
Renwick Olive

SW2814
Rookwood
Antique Gold

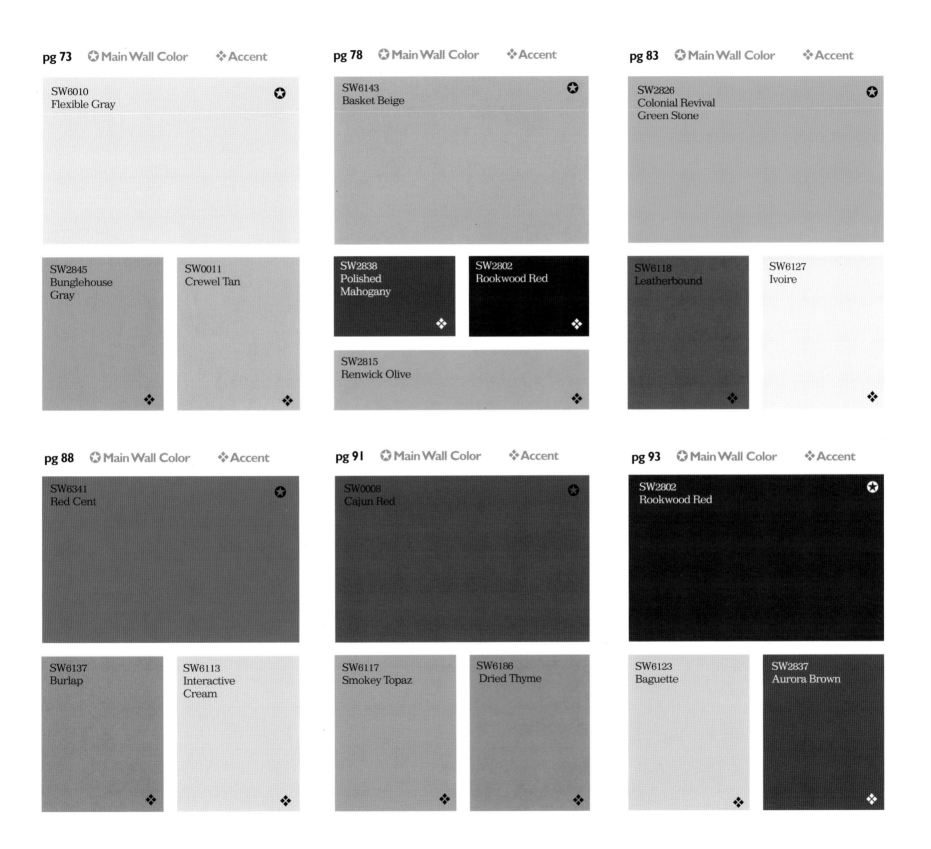

pg 73 ⭐ Main Wall Color ❖ Accent

SW6010
Flexible Gray ⭐

SW2845
Bunglehouse
Gray ❖

SW0011
Crewel Tan ❖

pg 78 ⭐ Main Wall Color ❖ Accent

SW6143
Basket Beige ⭐

SW2838
Polished
Mahogany ❖

SW2802
Rookwood Red ❖

SW2815
Renwick Olive ❖

pg 83 ⭐ Main Wall Color ❖ Accent

SW2826
Colonial Revival
Green Stone ⭐

SW6118
Leatherbound ❖

SW6127
Ivoire ❖

pg 88 ⭐ Main Wall Color ❖ Accent

SW6341
Red Cent ⭐

SW6137
Burlap ❖

SW6113
Interactive
Cream ❖

pg 91 ⭐ Main Wall Color ❖ Accent

SW0008
Cajun Red ⭐

SW6117
Smokey Topaz ❖

SW6186
Dried Thyme ❖

pg 93 ⭐ Main Wall Color ❖ Accent

SW2802
Rookwood Red ⭐

SW6123
Baguette ❖

SW2837
Aurora Brown ❖

pg 95 ⭐ Main Wall Color ❖ Accent

SW6125
Craft Paper ⭐

SW6107
Nomadic Desert ❖

SW6156
Ramie ❖

SW6048
Terra Brun ❖

pg 96 ⭐ Main Wall Color ❖ Accent

SW6083
Sable ⭐

SW6116
Tatami Tan ❖

SW6046
Swing Brown ❖

SW2827
Colonial Revival
Stone ❖

pg 100 ⭐ Main Wall Color ❖ Accent

SW6148
Wool Skein ⭐

SW6017
Intuitive ❖

SW0010
Wickerwork ❖

pg 105 ⭐ Main Wall Color ❖ Accent

SW6148
Wool Skein ⭐

SW6127
Ivoire ❖

SW6015
Vaguely Mauve ❖

pg 110 ⭐ Main Wall Color ❖ Accent

SW0070
Pink Shadow ⭐

SW6023
Insightful Rose ❖

SW6296
Fading Rose ❖

pg 114 ⭐ Main Wall Color ❖ Accent

SW6302
Innocence ⭐

SW6031
Glamour ❖

SW6050
Abalone Shell ❖

SHERWIN-WILLIAMS COLORS MATCHED TO GRAPHICS

pg 2

SW6033
Rembrandt Ruby

pg 2

SW6373
Harvester

pg 2

SW6121
Whole Wheat

pg 2

SW6643
Yam

pg 3

SW6823
Brave Purple

pg 3

SW6746
Julep

pg 3

SW6688
Solaria

pg 3

SW6913
Funky Yellow

pg 3

SW6831
Clematis

pg 3

SW6611
Jovial

pg 3

SW6485
Raindrop

pg 3

SW6659
Captivating Cream

pg 3

SW6779
Liquid Blue

pg 3

SW6258
Tricorn Black

pg 4

SW6485
Raindrop

pg 4

SW6484
Meander Blue

pg 17

SW6687
Lantern Light

pg 17

SW6653
Delicious Melon

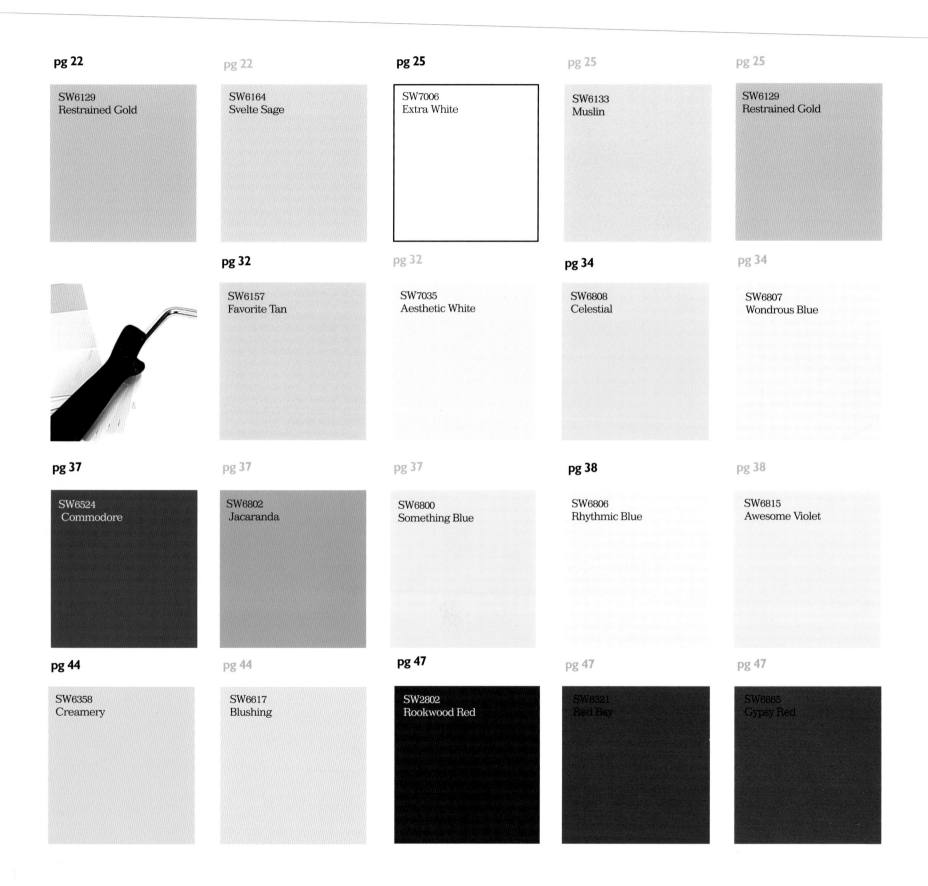

pg 22

SW6129
Restrained Gold

pg 22

SW6164
Svelte Sage

pg 25

SW7006
Extra White

pg 25

SW6133
Muslin

pg 25

SW6129
Restrained Gold

pg 32

SW6157
Favorite Tan

pg 32

SW7035
Aesthetic White

pg 34

SW6808
Celestial

pg 34

SW6807
Wondrous Blue

pg 37

SW6524
Commodore

pg 37

SW6802
Jacaranda

pg 37

SW6800
Something Blue

pg 38

SW6806
Rhythmic Blue

pg 38

SW6815
Awesome Violet

pg 44

SW6358
Creamery

pg 44

SW6617
Blushing

pg 47

SW2802
Rookwood Red

pg 47

SW6321
Red Bay

pg 47

SW6865
Gypsy Red

SHERWIN-WILLIAMS COLORS MATCHED TO GRAPHICS

pg 48

SW6060
Morrocan Brown

pg 48

SW6331
Smoky Salmon

pg 56

SW6146
Relaxed Khaki

pg 56

SW6371
Vanillin

pg 59

SW0012
Empire Gold

pg 59

SW6373
Harvester

pg 59

SW6687
Lantern Light

pg 60

SW6371
Vanillin

pg 60

SW6379
Jersey Cream

pg 66

SW6816
Dahlia

pg 66

SW6815
Awesome Violet

pg 69

SW6265
Quixotic Plum

pg 69

SW6557
Wood Violet

pg 69

SW6269
Beguiling Mauve

pg 70

SW6828
Rhapsody Lilac

pg 70

SW6830
Kismet

pg 76

SW6441
White Mint

pg 76

SW0042
Ruskin Room Green

pg **79**

SW6195
Rock Garden

pg 79

SW6179
Artichoke

pg 79

SW6715
Granita

pg **80**

SW6443
Relish

pg 80

SW6442
Supreme Green

pg **86**

SW6123
Baguette

pg 86

SW6120
Believable Buff

pg **89**

SW6062
Rugged Brown

pg 89

SW6349
Pennywise

pg 89

SW6653
Delicious Melon

pg **90**

SW0010
Wickerwork

pg 90

SW0079
Pinky Beige

pg **98**

SW6234
Uncertain Gray

pg 98

SW6232
Misty

pg **101**

SW6993
Black of Night

pg 101

SW7067
City Scape

pg 101

SW7064
Passive

pg **102**

SW7071
Gray Screen

pg 102

SW7072
Online

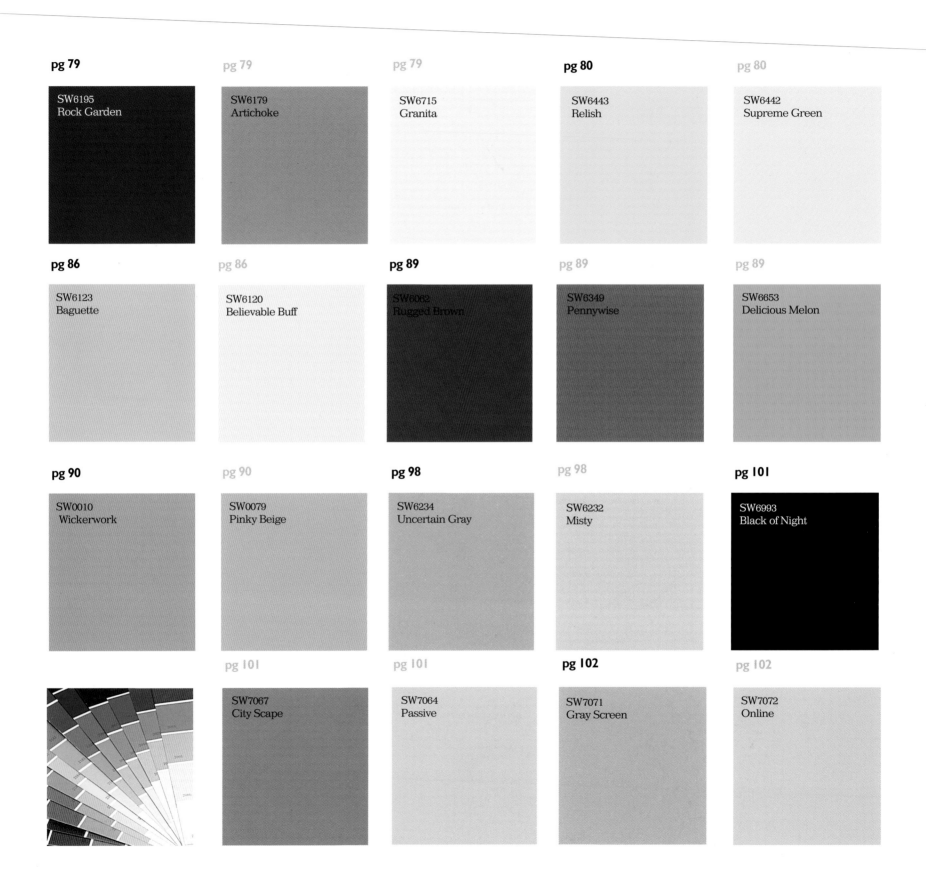

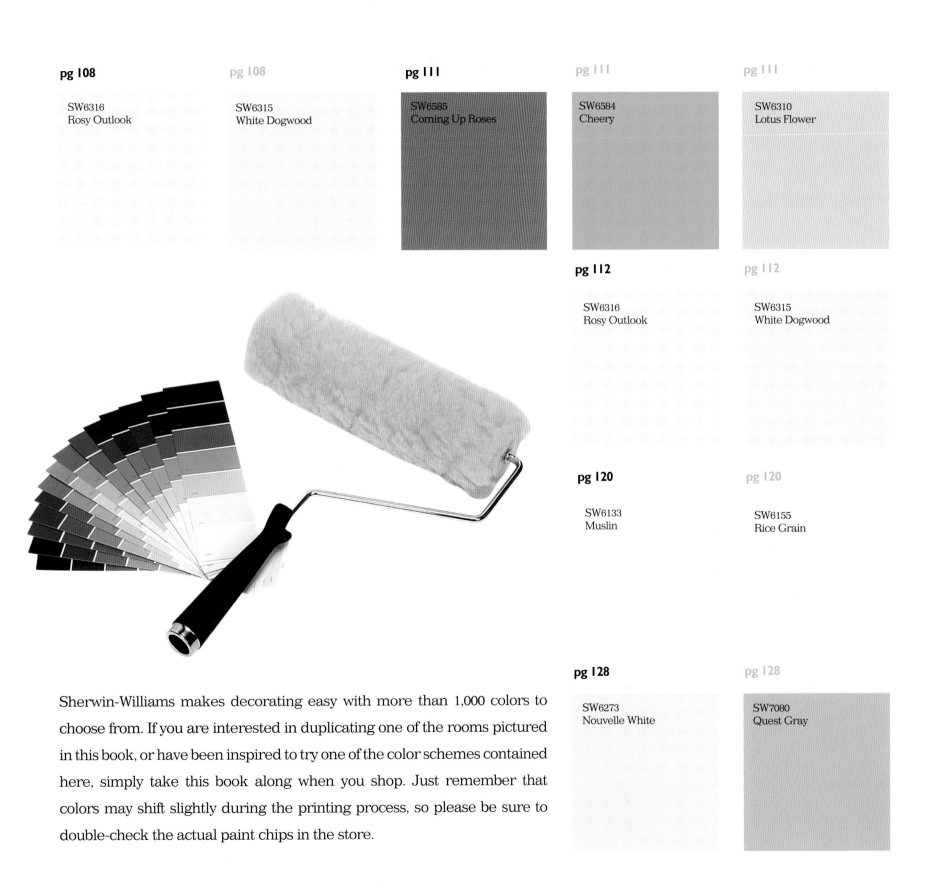

pg 108

SW6316
Rosy Outlook

pg 108

SW6315
White Dogwood

pg 111

SW6585
Coming Up Roses

pg 111

SW6584
Cheery

pg 111

SW6310
Lotus Flower

pg 112

SW6316
Rosy Outlook

pg 112

SW6315
White Dogwood

pg 120

SW6133
Muslin

pg 120

SW6155
Rice Grain

pg 128

SW6273
Nouvelle White

pg 128

SW7080
Quest Gray

Sherwin-Williams makes decorating easy with more than 1,000 colors to choose from. If you are interested in duplicating one of the rooms pictured in this book, or have been inspired to try one of the color schemes contained here, simply take this book along when you shop. Just remember that colors may shift slightly during the printing process, so please be sure to double-check the actual paint chips in the store.

ABOUT
THE AUTHOR

connie

Internationally recognized designer Connie Post is founder and chief executive of the Connie Post Companies, a portfolio of businesses well known in the trade as the leading design and strategic brand development firm in the home furnishings industry.

Armed with an uncanny understanding and compassion for women consumers ("When it comes to shopping, I can relate!" she says), Connie and her talented team have created exciting shopping environments for many of the most successful furniture retailers and manufacturers in the business. In fact, she's been personally responsible for the look and feel of some 16 million square feet of retail and wholesale space around the world.

Today, Connie is focused on sharing her unique message, "A beautiful room will change your life," and vast insider knowledge with women everywhere. To that end, she has created her own line of coordinated home furnishings products—Connie Post Collections—and as design spokesperson for a number of major retailers around the country, she educates shoppers about her Affordable Design™ concepts through newsletters, columns, books and seminars, as well as numerous television appearances.

"My goal is to preserve and protect the sanctity of home and point women back to their purpose," Connie says. "As a working Mom who raised two boys while simultaneously building a business, I'm all too familiar with the stressful, complex juggling act women contend with everyday. Home is our sanctuary and the center of family life, and it should be the one place in our lives where we love to be. Yet, rather than experiencing feelings of pride and joy when we survey our surroundings, too many feel only frustration, guilt and shame. Women instinctively want to create a comfortable and aesthetically pleasing environment for themselves and those they love, but the majority don't know where to begin and don't have time to figure it out. And, everybody is afraid of making a costly decorating mistake. I want to make creating a beautiful home fast, easy, affordable and fun."

For more information about Connie Post, visit www.conniepost.com.

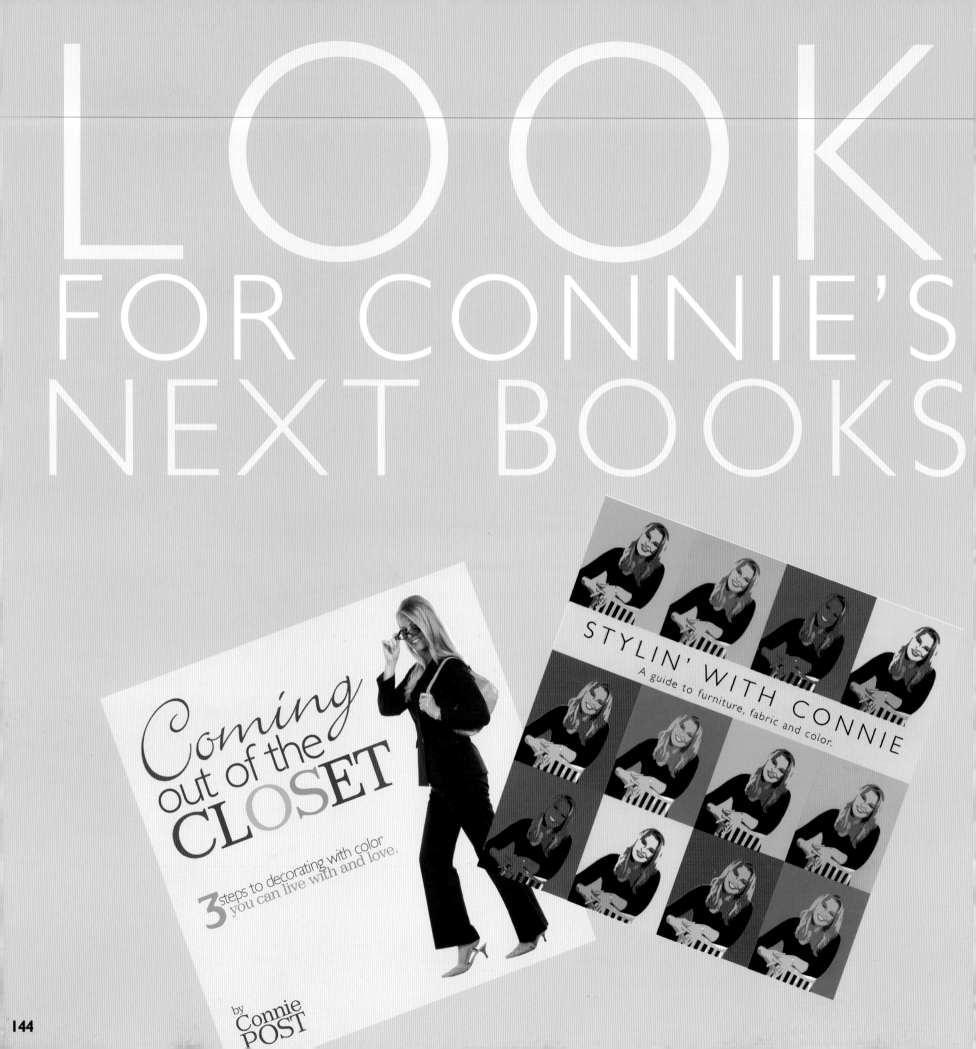

LOOK
FOR CONNIE'S
NEXT BOOKS

Coming out of the CLOSET

3 steps to decorating with color you can live with and love.

by Connie POST

STYLIN' WITH CONNIE
A guide to furniture, fabric and color.

144

LOOK FOR CONNIE'S
NATURALLY BEAUTIFUL FOR HOME & FAMILY
CLEANING PRODUCTS COMING SOON TO A STORE NEAR YOU.

Naturally Beautiful For Home & Family is a line of environmentally and body-friendly home care products featuring high-quality, all-natural cleaning ingredients infused with essential oils. Completely natural and toxin free, the aromatherapy-based line has been designed to clean your home and positively impact your senses and emotions.

The Clean Home Collection is pretty in pink on purpose. A portion of sales from the line will be donated to the City of Hope Cancer Center for breast cancer research. In other words, A Naturally Beautiful room will change lives!

dedication

This book is dedicated to my sons, Nathan and Seth, who have been my inspiration and my reason for getting out of bed every day and doing what I do. Special thanks to my entire creative staff at the Connie Post Companies for their continued hard work and commitment, and to Irv Blumkin, Robert Finger, Michael Kuhn, and especially John Klein who was the first to recognize that I was more than a pretty face in a prom dress.